HOW TO MASTER THE SCHOOL UNIVERSE: HOMEWORK, TEACHERS, TESTS, BULLIES, AND OTHER WAYS TO SURVIVE THE CLASSROOM

by Brooks Whitney

SCHOLASTIC INC.

New York Toronto London Auckland Sydney
Mexico City New Delhi Hong Kong Buenos Aires

ISBN: 0-439-57902-3

Design: Julie Mullarkey Gnoy
Illustrations: Kelly Kennedy

Copyright © 2004 by Scholastic Inc.

All rights reserved. Published by Scholastic Inc.

SCHOLASTIC, HOW TO SURVIVE ANYTHING, and associated logos are
trademarks and/or registered trademarks of Scholastic Inc.

12 11 10 9 8 7   6 7 8 9/0

Printed in the U.S.A.

First Scholastic printing, March 2004

CONTENTS

How to Survive This Book

What do you want to be when you grow up—a rocket scientist, veterinarian, writer, artist, spy, marine biologist, architect, photographer, banker, physician? Whatever it is you dream of becoming, **school is your ticket for getting there!** So even though school may sometimes seem like a total pain, believe it or not, it's one of the most important things you'll ever do. And since you *have* to go to school (it's your day job!), you might as well make the most of it!

That's where this book comes in handy. No matter what type of student you are, this book will help you **survive** each day by making it easier and more enjoyable. So if you're ready to **master school** and **have fun** at the same time, you've come to the right place! If you're psyched to learn how to tackle **tough tests**, do better in class, and **make the most of homework** so you have more free time, keep reading! Packed with simple tips to help you survive even the ickiest, stickiest school situations, this book is your "how-to" guide for surviving just about anything that might come your way!

You'll learn ways to make the most of your **study space**, why getting organized can help you get better grades, and tips for handling **cheaters** and **bullies**! If writing is your weak point, or the thought of giving an oral report gives you the jitters, you'll find solutions for that stuff, too—along with **cool research ideas** and tips for **presenting the perfect paper**.

You'll find charts, checklists, games, brainy recipes, and fun quizzes to help you learn more about your **student style**. And you'll find answers for how to deal with **embarrassing school situations** and what to do if you have a **mean teacher** or **forgot to do your homework**.

But school isn't just about teachers, grades, classes, and books. School is about meeting **new kids**, making **friends**, trying out for **plays** and **sports teams**, and joining **clubs**. It's about **discovering** what you like to do and the things you're good at—as you'll see in this book.

To help keep you organized and on top of your schoolwork, *How to Master the School Universe* also comes with a cool **Personal Digital Assistant (PDA)**. Here's a list of all the things it has and can do for you:

- ✔ a **clock** to help you keep track of time— no matter where in the world you are
- ✔ the **date**, in case you forget
- ✔ a **schedule** for keeping track of your classes, practices, and appointments
- ✔ an **alarm** to tell you when time's up
- ✔ a **memo pad** so you can write down things you need to do, and record homework assignments
- ✔ a **phone book** (in telephone mode) for storing names, e-mail addresses, and phone numbers
- ✔ a **calculator** to help you solve tough math problems
- ✔ **secret memory** for storing your most private and personal information
- ✔ a **metric converter** for translating feet into meters and vice versa

Read the *PDA Instruction Booklet* to learn how to use all the various functions. Whenever you see the **PDA** pictured in these pages, it means that you can use your PDA to help you.

With this book, your PDA, and an A+ attitude, you'll find school easier, more manageable, and even more fun!

TEN GREAT THINGS ABOUT SCHOOL

Who says school is all work and no fun?
Here's a list of things that make school cool...

1. Seeing friends

2. Snow days

3. Laughing at lunch

4. Learning something amazing

5. Understanding something you didn't before

6. Recess

7. Field trips

8. Discovering what you like to do

9. Figuring out what you're good at

10. Summer vacation

GO SCHOOL!

YEA TEAM!

TEN NOT-SO-GREAT THINGS ABOUT SCHOOL— AND WAYS TO MAKE THEM BETTER!

OK, so school's not *all* fun. Here's a list of things that can be a drag—and solutions to help you survive them!

1. Homework! *See page 61.*

2. Really long reading assignments. *See page 67.*

3. Studying. *See page 39.*

4. Taking tests. *See page 47.*

5. Writing papers. *See page 68.*

6. Cheaters. *See page 36.*

7. Being called on when you don't know the answer. *See page 23.*

8. Getting the jitters before your class presentation. *See page 32.*

9. Feeling stupid because you don't "get it." *See page 37.*

10. When you don't get the part in the play. *See page 53.*

Do you try your hardest to do well in school, or do you just try to slip by? Read the questions below and circle the answers that describe you best (be honest)!

1. Your teacher assigns a big history report that's due in three weeks. With so much time, you figure you can wait a week or two before starting and still have plenty of time to get it done right.

- **a.** Yep, that's me
- **b.** Sometimes that's me
- **c.** I wouldn't do that

2. When working on your history report, you figure you can save time with a one-stop shop and get all your info out of an encyclopedia.

- **a.** Yep, that's me
- **b.** Sometimes that's me
- **c.** I wouldn't do that

3. When taking a test, you decide it's a waste of time to do a quick review to see what's ahead and to identify trouble spots. Instead, you start at the beginning and work problem by problem.

- **a.** Yep, that's me
- **b.** Sometimes that's me
- **c.** I wouldn't do that

4. During the test, you get stuck on the essay question. Even though it's taking much more time than you'd expected, and you know you'd be better at the multiple-choice questions, you stick with it.

- **a.** Yep, that's me
- **b.** Sometimes that's me
- **c.** I wouldn't do that

5. Your favorite movie is on TV, but you still have a lot of reading to do. You decide to compromise and do your reading—but have the TV on in the background.

- **a.** Yep, that's me
- **b.** Sometimes that's me
- **c.** I wouldn't do that

6. You sit down to do your reading and realize that your highlighter has dried up. No big deal. You decide that you don't really need it anyway since you're sure to remember the important stuff.

- **a.** Yep, that's me
- **b.** Sometimes that's me
- **c.** I wouldn't do that

7. Your best friend is begging you to let them cheat off you during the spelling test. You agree to let them do it—you figure, just this once!

    a. Yep, that's me
    b. Sometimes that's me
    c. I wouldn't do that

8. Even though you're on the soccer team, play in the jazz band, and take trumpet lessons after school, you decide to try out for the school play, too. If you can't get your homework done before bed, you can always do it on the bus in the morning.

    a. Yep, that's me
    b. Sometimes that's me
    c. I wouldn't do that

9. When you get a test or assignment back with a not-so-great grade, you throw it in your book bag without a second thought.

    a. Yep, that's me
    b. Sometimes that's me
    c. I wouldn't do that

10. Your teacher is showing the class a math problem at the board and it seems like everyone in the class "gets it" but you. You decide to keep quiet and try to figure out the math problem by yourself later.

    a. Yep, that's me
    b. Sometimes that's me
    c. I wouldn't do that

REPORT CARD

Give yourself two points for every **c** you circled, and one point for every **b**. Give yourself zero points for every **a**.

☐ **Super Student (14–20 points)** From good time management, to smart study strategies, your actions show that you take school seriously. Your smart school sense is sure to bring success. Read this book to get tips on how to polish your A+ skills even further!

☐ **Satisfactory Student (8–13 points)** There's still room for improvement. A little more effort on your part could help you get better grades! Read on and make sure to note the sections that you're still struggling with.

☐ **S.O.S—Save Our Student! (0–7 points)** It looks like you need some help! No worries—read on for some super strategies to help you make the grade!

Before the Bell R-r-r-r-ings!

Y ou can help yourself do better in school before you even walk through the door! No books, no teachers, no studying—just a little time spent getting *yourself* organized. Are you drowning under piles of old papers and dried-up pens? Do you have **too much to do** and **not enough time** to do it? Read on to find out why **getting it together** at home can make a big difference in how you do in school!

GET READY!

Whether it's the beginning of the school year, somewhere in the middle, or almost the end, it's never too late to make a fresh start. From **organizing** your study space at home to getting the **school supplies** you need, a few simple preparations will help you a lot!

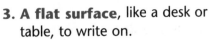

SPACE PLACE

All students need a **good study space**—a special spot where your mind clicks into study mode when you sit there. When choosing your space, make sure it has:

1. **Quiet.** Pick a place that isn't near a TV or in the center of everything else happening at home.

2. **Good light**, so you don't strain your eyes. Natural light from a window is considered best, but a bright lamp works great, too (and you'll need that at night, anyway!).

3. **A flat surface**, like a desk or table, to write on.

4. **A straight-backed chair**. It should be comfortable, but not so comfy that you fall asleep!

TRASH IT!

De-junking will help you unclutter your brain. Clean out your backpack, old folders, and desk drawers. Trash stuff that no longer works or serves a purpose, like dried-up pens, pencil stubs, worn-out erasers, crusty white out, and candy wrappers.

Bright Idea!

Scavenger Junk Hunt

Are you a **pack rat** or **neat freak**? Challenge yourself to a special Scavenger Hunt and find out! Write down a list of all the old, useless things you could possibly find buried deep in your desk drawers, old folders, and book bag. Now go on a hunt and find them! When you find an item on your list, check it off, then trash it. You may be surprised at what you uncover!

STORE IT!

Keep any old papers, reports, or tests you want to save in a pocket folder. Write on the front of the folder what's inside.

OLD PAPERS FROM MS. FORD'S SCIENCE CLASS

SCHOOL TOOLS

Doctors, dentists, architects, construction workers, chefs, and lots of other professions all have special tools to help them succeed at their jobs. Make a list of the supplies you'll need to help yourself get your job done, like...

❑ paper

❑ pencils and erasers, pens, markers

❑ pencil sharpener

❑ assignment book

❑ folders

❑ notebooks

❑ binders

❑ dictionary

❑ sticky notes

❑ stapler and staples

❑ tape

❑ scissors

❑ ruler

❑ computer

❑ PDA

Personal Digital Assistant

Your **PDA** can help you get organized! Here's how...

1. Use the **schedule** function to keep track of your class schedule, due dates, appointments, birthdays, special events, and vacations.

2. Store e-mail addresses and phone numbers in the **phone book** (in telephone mode).

3. Write down any school supplies you need to get in the **memo pad**.

Places, Please!

Once you've de-junked, **get organized**. Use everyday household items to help you clean up the clutter and organize your study space.

Silverware Divider: You're used to seeing these inside kitchen drawers, keeping silverware organized, but they work great for organizing school supplies, too. Put markers in one space, colored pencils in another, your ruler in the next, and so on. Either slip the divider into your desk drawer, or keep it on the table within easy reach while you're doing your homework.

Junior Jars: Small jars, like those used for baby food, are perfect for storing paper clips, staples, spare change, and other small stuff you want to keep track of. And they fit neatly into a drawer! To remove the label, soak the empty jar in hot, soapy water until it comes off. Use a sponge to scrub off any sticky stuff.

Box It: Store extra paper, magazines, and school handouts in recycled cereal boxes. When the cereal is gone, throw out the inside bag and cut off the top flaps. Cut the box diagonally on both sides. Decorate with wrapping paper or make a collage by gluing on pictures cut out of magazines.

Pocket Stuffers: Hanging shoe holders have lots of pockets for storing lots of stuff—other than shoes! From paints and paint brushes, to stationery, notepads, rolls of tape, and jars of glue, there's a place for everything. Hang the shoe holder in your closet to keep it out of the way.

GET SET!

Now that your stuff is organized, do you yourself have it together? **Taking care of yourself** may not seem like it has much to do with how you do in school, but it does! Read on for a few simple tips that will help you feel great throughout the Monday-Friday day.

GET A GOOD NIGHT'S SLEEP

When you're tired, it means your brain is tired, too. Having a **tired brain** makes for a very long school day! It's harder to pay attention, think smart, and participate. You're more likely to space out, yawn loudly while the teacher's talking, and stare at the clock for long periods of time. To combat sleepy-student syndrome, try to get eight hours of sleep a night. **Being well-rested will help you stay sharp!**

EAT (A HEALTHY) BREAKFAST

Studies show that kids who eat breakfast do better in school. It makes sense—who can concentra on math problems and geography tests with a rumbling stomach an brain filled with thoughts of lunch **Food is fuel**. Use it to power you body and brain *before* you head o the door. And if you bag your lun don't forget to take it with you!

Brainy Breakfasts

Try these quickie breakfasts that
you can grab on the go!

Sunrise Smoothies

Mix a glass of orange juice, half a
container of vanilla yogurt, a banana
chopped into pieces, and four ice
cubes in a blender. Blend on high until everything is mixed up
and frothy. Slurp your way to school!

Scoop It Up!

Mix up a batch of this crunchy morning meal on wheels.
Scoop into a resealable plastic bag, grab a carton of juice
or milk, and go!

Add 1 cup of all these ingredients together and shake it up.

- mixed nuts like almonds, cashews, pistachios, and pecans
- raisins or dried cranberries
- yogurt-covered raisins or nuts
- granola, oat or rice cereal (or any of your other faves)
- shredded coconut

P, B, & J Waffle-wich

Toast two frozen waffles, then spread with peanut butter and
jelly. Put them together to make a sandwich.

It's a Wrap!

To make this breakfast burrito, roll up your favorite ingredients
in a tortilla and microwave (with a grown-up's help) for 20
seconds, until it's all gooey and good! Here are a few to try:

- cream cheese & jelly • peanut butter & banana
- sliced apple and raisins drizzled with honey

Pizza Bagels Pizza for breakfast!

Toast a bagel, then spread each half with catsup or tomato
sauce and top with a slice of cheese. Pop the bagel, open face,
in the toaster oven until the cheese melts.

PUT YOURSELF TOGETHER

Being put together isn't about wearing the latest styles or having the biggest wardrobe. It's simply about taking the time to put yourself together! What does your appearance say about you? Do you look like you just **rolled out of bed**, or are you **neat and tidy**, ready to master the school universe instead? Just like your folks put themselves together for work, you should do the same for school. And just like being in your pajamas helps you get ready for sleep, putting yourself together will help your mind click into school mode.

Go!

An airplane pilot goes through a series of checks before take-off, and so should you! From homework assignments to the right folder and books, you can do better in school by simply *not* forgetting important stuff! It only takes a couple of minutes to make sure you have everything you need.

CHECK POINT — Before Taking Off for School

Make sure you have:

✔ books

✔ plenty of paper, your notebooks, sharpened pencils, and a few pens

✔ finished homework

✔ lunch or lunch money

✔ signed permission slips

✔ house keys

School Daze! Surviving Life in the Classroom

Most of what you learn takes place in the classroom. So it's smart to know how to **listen** and how to **take notes**. Your **attitude counts** for something, too. Teachers are impressed by students who try! Think about it: do you participate in class discussion? Sit where you can see the board? Keep quiet when your teacher is speaking? These are all things that can affect your grade. Keep reading to learn how to make the most of class time!

TEN WAYS TO DO BETTER IN CLASS WITHOUT EVEN CRACKING A BOOK

1. Make sure you have everything you need *before* class starts

2. Be on time

3. Write down all your assignments so you don't forget anything

4. Turn things in when you're supposed to

5. Speak up! Taking part in class discussions can improve your grade

6. Don't talk while your teacher's talking

7. Ask if you don't understand

8. Take the time to go over assignments and tests *before* turning them in

9. Write neatly so your teacher can read your work

10. Listen up!

BE ON TIME.

DON'T TALK WHILE MS. BURT'S TALKING.

HOW DO YOU LEARN BEST?

Everyone has a *style* of learning that works best for them. Whether it's one specific style or a combination, **knowing what works for you** will help you learn info and remember it. Answer the questions below to help you discover your special learning style (it's OK to have more than one answer)!

1. When putting something together, like a model airplane or a new toy, it's easiest for you if you

   a. read the directions and look at the diagram

   b. hear the directions read out loud

   c. jump right in and start working with someone who knows how to do it

2. When learning to play a new board game, it's easiest for you to

   a. read the directions

   b. hear the directions read out loud

   c. start playing the game and learn as you go

3. When making chocolate chip cookies, it's easiest for you to

   a. read the directions

   b. hear the directions read out loud

   c. make cookies with someone and learn as you go

4. When learning to play a new sport, it's easiest for you to learn by

   a. watching the game being played

   b. hearing the directions explained

   c. playing and learning as you go

5. When making something new in art class, it's easiest for you if you

    a. watch your teacher do it first

    b. listen to your teacher explain it

    c. start experimenting until you get it right

6. When playing a video game for the first time, it's easiest for you if you

    a. read the directions

    b. listen as your friend reads them out loud

    c. start playing and learn as you go

Answer Key

There is no right or wrong, only what works for you! Review the quiz and add up how many times you circled each letter. Then check below for the style—or styles—that help you learn best.

If you circled mostly A...

SEEING is believing. If you can get your "eyes" on the info—words, diagrams, movies, maps, pictures—your brain will process it. Turn to the **Study Smarter** section on pages 40–41 for tips on putting your study style to work.

If you circled mostly B...

HEARING helps you remember. From listening to class talks, to reading out loud, and to playing the radio, your brain tunes in when your ears do. Turn to the **Study Smarter** section on pages 40–41 for tips on putting your study style to work.

If you circled mostly C...

DOING it gets the info to sink in for you. Touching, moving, acting it out, writing, experimenting—for you, hands-on means your head's on, too! Turn to the **Study Smarter** section on pages 40–41 for tips on putting your study style to work.

BODY LANGUAGE

When you're sitting in class, what do your actions say about your 'tude? Take a look at the pictures below. Now put *yourself* in the picture and think of what your body language might say to your teacher!

SURVIVAL TIP:

Actions can speak just as loud as words! The actions of the kids in the pictures above shout out "I DON'T CARE ABOUT WHAT YOU'RE TEACHING!" This is *not* a good message to be giving to your teacher. If you have a problem staying focused during class, see page 21 for ways to help you tune in your teacher and tune out the distractions.

LISTEN UP!

Did you know that most of the info you learn is presented orally by your teacher in class? That's why being a **good listener** is important to your success in school. Check out the listening tips below and learn some basic ways to **concentrate better** on what's being said.

FOCUS

Keep your eyes on the person who is talking. It'll help you stay focused.

SHAKE IT UP

Are you starting to nod off in class? Spacing out for long periods of time? Move a little. That's right, squirm in your seat. Sit up straighter. Roll your shoulders. Wiggle your fingers and toes. Give your head a little shake to clear it. Take a deep breath. Now that your body and brain are awake, tune back in to the speaker.

NOTE THIS

Take notes. It will make you a more active listener. Writing things down also reinforces what you hear and helps you to remember. For more note-taking tips, check out **Take Note!** on page 24.

ONE THING AT A TIME

It's very difficult to listen *and* do something else at the same time.

PICTURE IT!

Try to create a picture in your head of what's being said. If your teacher's reading a short story out loud to the class, try to imagine the characters in action.

PARTICIPATE

Make an effort to take part in the class discussion. Staying involved will help you stay awake!

Tune In

Did you know that **listening** and **hearing** are not the same thing? *Hearing* simply means the words are entering your ears. *Listening* means that you are thinking about them and trying to understand and remember their meaning.

Blooper!

"Sometimes my teacher calls on me even when I'm not raising my hand. If I get the answer wrong, the whole class laughs."

1. Kids who laugh at other kids when they answer a question wrong aren't very nice. People often laugh at others because they are feeling insecure. Perhaps they didn't know the answer either and are relieved they weren't in the hot seat—this time!

2. Remind yourself that even the *best* students answer questions wrong. That's why you go to school—to learn! If you had all the answers, you wouldn't need school!

3. Make sure you're prepared when you go to class. Did you do your homework? Did you review your notes?

Sometimes teachers call on students who *aren't* raising their hand because they don't participate very much on their own. To keep yourself out of a potentially embarrassing situation, take the initiative and raise your hand for questions you *do* know the answer to!

TAKE NOTE!

Good note-taking is a skill that comes with practice. You don't want to have too little written down—or too much! Smart notes will make studying for tests a much simpler task. Here's a list of things to do to help you get the job done.

1. Write the **date** and **subject** at the top of the page. The date will serve as a good reference when you want to compare notes with friends. It'll also remind you of any days that you missed and need to get notes for.

2. Listen for the **important stuff**. You don't have time to write down *everything* your teacher says, so keep your ears open for the five W's: **Who, What, Where, When,** and **Why.**

3. **Shorten** words and sentences. Save time by using **abbreviations** or make up your own shorthand. Be careful not to make your shorthand so short you can't figure out the original word you were trying to abbreviate!

4. Put a **question mark** next to anything you didn't understand or didn't finish writing down. It'll help you remember to ask a friend or teacher later.

5. **Underline, circle, or put a star** next to anything the teacher **repeats** or **emphasizes**. That usually means it's Very Important Information!

6. Write down any **questions** your teacher asks. That's usually a good hint that it's important and will probably show up on a test.

Date and Subject

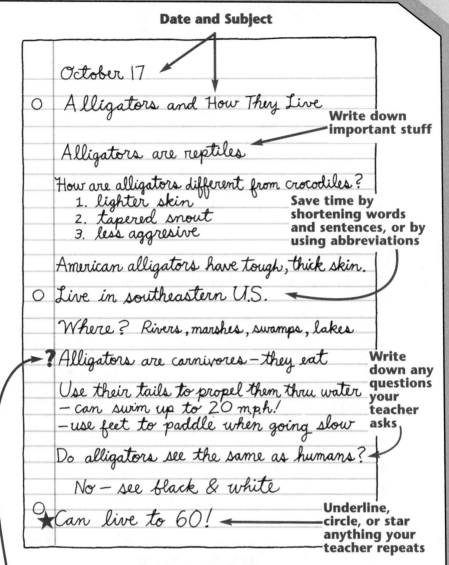

October 17

○ Alligators and How They Live

Write down important stuff

Alligators are reptiles

How are alligators different from crocodiles?
1. lighter skin
2. tapered snout
3. less aggresive

Save time by shortening words and sentences, or by using abbreviations

American alligators have tough, thick skin.

○ Live in southeastern U.S.

Where? Rivers, marshes, swamps, lakes

? Alligators are carnivores — they eat

Write down any questions your teacher asks

Use their tails to propel them thru water
— can swim up to 20 m.p.h.!
— use feet to paddle when going slow

Do alligators see the same as humans?

No — see black & white

○ ★ Can live to 60!

Underline, circle, or star anything your teacher repeats

Put a question mark by anything you didn't understand or didn't finish writing down

Missed Notes

If you're having trouble keeping up and are worried that you're missing important stuff, ask your teacher if you can bring a small tape recorder to class to help you record the class info. When you get home, listen to the tape and review your notes to make sure you didn't miss anything. If you did, write it down.

Blooper!

"I was walking to the front of the room to write on the chalkboard and I accidentally farted...loud enough for the whole class to hear!"

1. Horror of horrors—it just slipped out, and everyone knows it's you. Don't try to deny it, you're sure to create a bigger scene when all you really want to do is have people stop looking at you!

2. Politely say, "excuse me" like it's no big deal—because it's really not! (Everyone does it!)

3. Even though your face is burning and the class is howling, do your best to ignore them and focus on something else, like doing your problem at the board.

4. Sure, it's kind of gross, but it's *natural*. Remember that every kid in your class does it, too!

5. When class gets out, find some friends and let them comfort you. Hopefully, you'll be able to get a good laugh out of the silly situation and then forget about it. The rest of the class will, too.

Laugh At Yourself!

It makes you look confident even when you're not feeling confident. If you turn your mortifying moments into harmless jokes by laughing about them, people are less likely to make fun of you! After all, why would they bother to poke fun at you when you've already made fun of yourself? Remind yourself that what makes you cringe today will probably make you laugh in a couple of days—and turn it into a pretty funny story to tell, as well!

THE KEY TO PUTTING TOGETHER A WINNING GROUP PROJECT? TEAMWORK!

Group projects are actually a lot like playing a **team sport**. In order to succeed, **everyone needs to play a part**, try their hardest, and work together to achieve a common goal. Whether you're working on a science project with a couple of classmates, or writing a play for English class with a bigger group, here are some tips to help you get your team together and going strong!

TEAM CAPTAIN

It's a good idea to pick a **group leader** to help keep everything together. The group leader should be responsible for writing down what everyone's job is, keeping notes, and marking important dates, like meetings and due dates, in a calendar. Being group leader doesn't mean being the boss!

HUDDLE!

Put your heads together and **brainstorm** until you agree on your goal. Brainstorming means coming up with a big list of ideas. It's important to be accepting of everyone's ideas and not make others feel bad if you don't like their suggestions. Once you have a list, narrow it down to the group's top two or three favorites and take a vote.

MAKE A GAME PLAN

Now that the group has a goal, follow these four steps for creating a plan to get it done!

To Do List

1) Make a list of all the things you need to do.

2) Rank the things in the order they should be completed.

3) Set deadlines for finishing each part of the project.

4) Divide up the work and give everyone a job to do.

HALF TIME

Meet as a group from time to time and check up on everyone's progress. Is everyone doing their part? Is the group still on schedule? Does a group member need help? These are all good things to go over.

SO WE SHOULD HAVE OUR OUTLINE BY TOMORROW....

PRACTICE

If your group is actually going to be presenting something to the class, **practice** before you **perform**! It can only make the presentation better.

SCORE!

Every good athlete knows that winning takes **teamwork**. So does a good group project. A group is a powerful thing. Separately, each member can only carry so much weight, but together you can move mountains!

SURVIVAL TIP:

Everyone has their own opinions and ideas. In order for a group to work as a team, you have to be willing to **compromise**. Sometimes you have to bend your ideas to fit somebody else's. If everyone insisted on doing things their own way, nothing would get done!

Referee, Please!

What to Do When...

The Group Just Can't Agree

Making decisions as a group can be tough—especially since it's unlikely that everyone will agree on the same thing! It's OK to disagree. The important thing is how you resolve it. Start by having a group discussion. Let each member give their opinion. Now can the group agree? If not, take a vote.

Group Members Don't Do Their Share

Is there a slacker in the pack? It's not fair if someone is relying on the rest of the group to do all the work. Have a group meeting and review what each person's job is. Ask the person who *isn't* helping if there's a reason they haven't done their share. Do they need help? If the person still isn't willing to pitch in, get a teacher's help. After all, that's what the teacher is there for!

GREAT PRESENTATIONS

Giving an **oral report** is like putting on a one-man (or -woman) show. You'll need to **prepare, practice,** and **perform**. It's your job to both inform and keep your audience interested. Follow these tips to help you put on a star performance!

PREPARE

Preparing an oral report is similar to preparing a written report. Unless the topic has been assigned, you should **choose a subject** that's interesting to you. What do you care about or want to learn more about? **Follow your interests** and you'll find your topic. For brainstorming tips, see page 69.

RESEARCH!

It's important to really know your subject. Use a variety of sources to help you find engaging and informative facts. For research tips, visit page 70.

PUT IT TOGETHER

Just like a written report, an oral report has **three basic sections**:

The Introduction introduces your subject. It should also hook your audience by catching their interest. Try opening with a thought-provoking question, interesting fact, true story, or personal experience that relates to your topic.

The Body is the main part of your report, and will use most of your time. If you were listening to a report on your subject, what would you want to know? Too much information can seem overwhelming, and too little can be confusing. Organize your outline around your key points and focus on getting them across. Use *visual aids*, like posters, maps, slides, or pictures, to help make your points and entertain your audience.

The Conclusion is the time to summarize and get across your most important point. What do you want the audience to remember?

PEEK SHEET

The last thing you want to do while giving your report is to stand in one place and *read it*. It's very hard to keep an audience interested if you do. For some students, writing out the entire report word for word, then transferring the main points to **note cards** they can glance at while speaking, works best. Others like to create an **outline** to guide them while speaking. Make sure you write BIG so you can read your notes at a glance, and don't use long sentences. Use **key words** or **short phrases** that will prompt you instead.

WHY CATS ARE FUN

STRING
BALLS
PLAYFUL

POP   POP   POP

REHEARSE

Practicing your report is key to your success! Rehearse in front of a mirror, speak into a tape recorder, or just stand alone in your room. **Time yourself** to make sure your report isn't too long or too short. When you're comfortable with your presentation, **practice on your family or a friend**. Be open to any tips or helpful hints they offer.

REPORT

It's show time! Almost everyone is **nervous** before speaking in front of a group. Being **well prepared** and **comfortable** with your info is the best way to combat nerves. Before you begin, take a deep breath to help calm your jitters. You may be nervous in the beginning, but once you get started, you're likely to feel more comfortable.

USE GESTURES

MAKE EYE CONTACT

USE YOUR VOICE

PACE YOURSELF

Try these tips to help you give a polished presentation!

- **Make eye contact.** It helps the audience feel involved. If you're feeling nervous, make eye contact with a friend. It's a lot better than staring at the floor or your notes!

- **Use gestures.** Your body language can help you make your points and keep the audience interested.

- **Use your voice.** Don't just babble on in the same tone, or mumble. Vary your tone and speak clearly.

- **Pace yourself.** When people get nervous, they tend to speed up their talking. If you find yourself hurrying, take a deep breath and slow down.

TROUBLE IN THE CLASSROOM

Yikes! It's not always going to be smooth sailing. From teacher troubles to tutors, to cheaters and teasers, the seas will get stormy. Don't panic! These what-to-do tips will help guide you into calmer seas.

POP QUIZ

TRUE OR FALSE: IS YOUR TEACHER MEAN?

Put a T for true or an F for false by each statement. Then check **Two Sides to Every Story** on page 34 to see what your answers say about your teacher—and you!

My teacher...

1. Gives really hard tests ☐

2. Picks on me in front of everyone ☐

3. Assigns too much homework ☐

4. Acts mad when I ask questions ☐

5. Yells at the class for no reason ☐

6. Doesn't accept late homework ☐

TWO SIDES TO EVERY STORY...

Just like there are two sides to every story, there are also two ways to look at a situation. There's your point of view, and your teacher's. Now read the statements on page 33 again here, along with the accompanying questions. You may see things through different eyes!

My teacher...

1. **Gives really hard tests**
   Does your teacher give hard tests because she's mean—or because she's trying to help you **learn**?

2. **Picks on me in front of everyone**
   Does your teacher pick on you because of the way you **act**? Stop for a moment and look at your own behavior. Do you talk while she's talking, yawn loudly, or get caught staring out the window instead of the blackboard?

3. **Assigns too much homework**
   Is your teacher assigning all that homework to make the class miserable—or perhaps because he wants you to **practice** what's been taught in class?

4. **Acts mad when I ask questions**
   Could your teacher be annoyed because you ask him to **repeat** things you would have heard if you'd been listening the first time?

5. **Yells at the class for no reason**
   Does your teacher really yell at the class for *no reason*? Something usually **prompts** it.

6. **Doesn't accept late homework**
   Rules are rules. Is your homework late for a good reason, like you were **sick**, or because you just didn't do it?

TALKING TO TEACHERS: THREE STRATEGIES FOR GETTING THE RESULTS YOU WANT!

Make it your goal to have a conversation, not a confrontation. Try the following strategies for getting what you want.

1. Be Polite

Don't say
"That's not fair! Why did I get a C?"

Do say
"Excuse me, Miss Brown, could I please talk to you after class?"

2. Don't Blame

Don't say
"Your tests are totally unfair!"

Do say
"That was a really hard test. Could we have a review session before the next one?"

3. Ask For Advice!

Don't say
"I don't get it!"

Do say
"Do you have any tips for getting this to sink in?"

THAT WAS A REALLY HARD TEST. COULD WE HAVE A REVIEW SESSION BEFORE THE NEXT ONE?

CLASSMATE TROUBLES

From competition to copycats, check
out these tips for surviving the tough stuff.

HELP! "I wish I were a better athlete…"

Not everyone can be good at everything, but **everyone is good at something!** So maybe you're not one of those kids who is a natural athlete, but that doesn't mean you can't find a sport that you can play and enjoy. Baseball, soccer, tennis, swimming, dance, field hockey, basketball, volleyball…there are lots to choose from! You might not be good at *all* of them, but you can surely learn to be good at *one* of them. You may never be the best player on the team, or in gym class, but as long as you have fun doing it, who cares?

HELP! When a friend distracts you in class by whispering in your ear and passing notes, or wanting to cheat…

Write a quick note back asking your friend to "please stop!" or quietly shake your head "no." After class, **talk to your friend** and tell her how you feel. Real friends won't hold it against you. If they act mad, tell them you're sorry they're upset. But you don't have to apologize for not joining in or agreeing to cheat!

HELP! Competition in the classroom

Do you ever feel **bummed out** that your friend gets **better grades** than you even though you study harder? Or find yourself feeling **jealous**? It can be frustrating to study super hard and have your friend still do better than you, even though he's barely cracked a book. The truth is, that no matter who you are or what you're good at, there's almost **always going to be someone** who does just **a little bit better**. Accept it and stop trying to compete with your friend so it doesn't ruin a good friendship. Next time you're feeling competitive, think about all the things that you're good at instead.

BRAIN BUSTERS

Yikes! Lots of kids feel pressure in the classroom. Some worry that they're stupid. Some worry that they're too smart. And some feel huge pressure to get good grades so they can please their parents. Read on for tips on what to do if one of those students is you!

HELP! "How come everyone understands but me?"

1. Everybody learns in different ways and at different speeds. Some people learn best when they hear the information, like a teacher speaking. Others learn best by reading, or seeing the information on a blackboard. And still others learn best by doing hands-on work, like science experiments. To find the **study style that works best for you**, turn to page 18. Whether it's one way or a combination, knowing what works best for you will help you take it all in and remember it.

2. Just as there are different ways to learn, there are also **different kinds of "smart."** Grades are not really a good measurement of how smart you are, but how well you've learned the info given to you in class. There are many very smart students who don't get very good grades! Perhaps they didn't study. Or maybe they study really hard but get terrible test anxiety. Some students may do well on multiple-choice questions and draw a big blank when it comes to essay questions. The important thing about whatever grade you get is that you tried your hardest.

3. **If you're really having trouble** tackling a certain subject, get help! The important thing is that you understand the stuff. In school, ideas tend to build on themselves. If you don't understand early on, chances are your confusion will grow until you're completely lost! Before that happens, talk to a parent or teacher about getting some **extra help**, like a **tutor** to work with you one-on-one.

HELP! Feeling too much pressure to achieve?

Where is the pressure coming from? Are you putting pressure on **yourself**, or is the pressure coming from a **parent or teacher**? A little pressure can be a good motivator, but too much can make you so stressed out that you can't do anything well! Here are a few things to remember:

1. Parents and teachers want you to **do your best**. As a result, they may push you to try harder because they think that you're not working up to your ability. If you feel that you *are*, talk to your parent or teacher and let them know this. They really want (or should want) to **help you, not hurt you**!

2. If you're putting **too much pressure on yourself**, you need to remember this: Very few students get A's in everything, and getting a B is certainly nothing to feel bad about! And believe it or not, it's not the grade that's the most important thing, but that you tried your best.

3. There's **more to school** than getting straight A's! School is a place for finding out what you like to do and trying out new ideas. A successful student is one who **works hard**, has many **interests, gets involved** in activities, and **has fun**! So don't judge your success as a student *only* by your academic performance. There's so much more to it!

HELP! How to survive being the class "smarty pants"

Do people make fun of you because you're *too* smart? Even though the teasing hurts, you have to remember that they're probably jealous. After all, who doesn't want to get good grades? As long as you aren't a show-off, classmates shouldn't hold your high scores against you. Be happy for what you're good at! (And find more friends like yourself!)

SURVIVAL TIP:
Practice + more practice = improvement!

Ace That Test!

Teachers use tests to find out how well you've learned the stuff they've been teaching. Instead of thinking of tests as horrible obstacles to survive, think of them as *challenges* to conquer! Before tackling any challenge, you need to prepare and practice. From **study strategies**, to **test-taking tips**, this section is full of ideas to help you survive the hard stuff so you can **ace that test!**

STUDY SMARTER

Unless you're a complete genius, you're going to have to prepare for tests and exams. There's no way around it (if there were, we'd be happy to say so!). That means **studying**. So make the most of the situation and follow these strategies to help you get the job done right—and even have fun doing it!

DO YOU KNOW <u>WHAT</u> TO STUDY?

1. Start by reviewing your **past tests and quizzes**. It will give you an idea of your teacher's test style. What kinds of questions does she ask? Where does she get most of her test questions from—is it from stuff taught in class, homework assignments, or readings? Use these clues to help predict what might be on your next test.

2. Review your **class notes**. Highlight any info that the teacher emphasized or repeated, and any questions she asked. Highlight any of the Five W's, too: **who, what, where, when**, and **why**. (For tips on taking great notes, turn to pages 24–25.)

3. Be sure to review past homework and reading assignments. You're likely to see much of this stuff resurface on the test. **Highlight** or **star** anything you need to study.

Remember the Study Style quiz you took on page 18? Here's your chance to put it to work. Look for the **eye**, **ear**, and **hand** symbols next to each idea to see if it matches your "study style."

  Making a study sheet is a good way to condense and organize important info. Along with reviewing the stuff, ask yourself questions and answer them out loud, too.

Columbus
Discovered America
1492
3 ships—Niña, Pinta
& Santa Maria
Died 1506

  **Flash cards**. Using index cards, write a question or term on the front, and the answer on the back. Now quiz yourself. If you get the answer right, put the card aside. If you're wrong, put the card on the bottom of the pile and try again.

When did Columbu discover America

 **Draw pictures**. Some people remember things best when they can see a picture in their mind. Add art to your *flash cards* or *study sheet* to serve as reminders. During the test, you might not remember the answer, but perhaps seeing the picture in your head will help jog your memory.

NIÑA   PINTA   SANTA MARIA

 Post it! Write important info on **sticky notes** and stick them in places you're sure to see them, like your closet door, bathroom mirror, or computer screen.

Read out loud your notes, homework assignments, or any other stuff you need to learn for the test. Hearing the info can help it stick in your mind.

 Make a tape. Record yourself reading your *study sheet* or *flash cards*. When you want to study, just hit play. You can listen to your tape on the bus to school, sitting under a tree at recess, or just before you take the test!

   Make a video. Pretend you're a news anchor and have someone videotape you explaining the info as if you were actually delivering the news. Not only will making the video help you learn, but watching it will, too!

  Chart it. Make timelines, diagrams, graphs, or charts as another way to organize and view info.

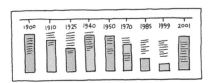

Make a sample test. Think of questions that your teacher might ask on the test and write them down. Use the test to test yourself, or swap sample tests with a study buddy and see how you do.

Bright Idea!

Flashcard Fun!

Try these games to liven up your study time. All you
need is a pack of index cards, your study materials,
and a study buddy or two.

Concentration

Come up with a list of 20
questions that could possibly be
on your test. Write each question
down on an index card. Now write
the answers down on another set
of index cards. Shuffle them
together and lay them out face
down in rows of four. Just like in
the card game, take turns picking
a card, and then trying to find its
match. Each player gets one

chance—if they miss, it's the next player's turn. If a match is
made, the player keeps the two cards, and goes again. At the
end, the player with the most cards wins.

Stumped!

Go through your study
materials and come up with
the ten hardest questions you
can think of. Write the
questions and answers on an
index card (one on each side).
Have a partner do the same.
Now take turns drawing a flash

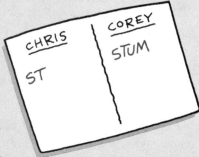

card from your opponent's pile and answering it.
If you answer the question incorrectly, you take a
letter from the word "stumped." The first player to
spell S-T-U-M-P-E-D is out.

Go to Jail

You'll need a Monopoly board for this game. Have each player come up with a list of questions that could possibly be on your test. Write each question down on an index card until you have 20 of them. Set up the Monopoly 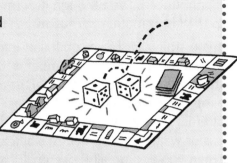 board and play following the regular directions. **Here's the twist—any time a player rolls doubles, the player must draw a flash card and answer the question correctly.** If the player is right, she moves ahead. If she's wrong, she goes directly to jail. Just like in the actual game, to get out of jail, you must roll doubles again—but this time, again, you have to draw a card and answer the question correctly! Otherwise, you must stay in jail!

Hangman

Have each player come up with a list of questions that could possibly be on your test. Write each question down on an index card until you have about 20 of them. Put them in a pile. Draw a hangman noose for each player. The first player draws a card and tries to answer the question. If the player is right, it's  the next person's turn. If the player is wrong, the player must add a body part to his drawing. The first person to get a head, body, arms, and legs is hung!

WHEN TO STUDY?

Give yourself plenty of time and start on the day the test is announced. Even though it's tempting to leave studying to the last minute, **cramming** isn't a good idea.

If you stuff your brain too full of info without giving it time to sink in, you won't remember it for long! Break your studying into **manageable bites** and tackle some **every day**. Make the most of small chunks of time, too, like while you're riding the bus or waiting in the dentist's office. When you add up all those small chunks of time spent studying, they actually equal a pretty big chunk! The best way to **memorize** something is to **see it again and again**. When the test day comes, the info should be absorbed into your brain and easy to access!

WHO TO STUDY WITH?

Some students like to study alone. Others like to work with a **classmate** or in a **study group**. There's no right or wrong way, just what works for you. Here are some things to consider.

Study Buddies

Two heads can sometimes be better than one. Studying with a friend, or in a study group, can be helpful because:

1. It will help you make—and stick to—a study schedule

2. You can compare notes to see if you missed any info

3. There's someone to explain what you don't understand

4. You can learn new study techniques—maybe they have a trick you don't know

5. You can quiz each other

Time Out!

Don't let your study buddy become a **distraction**. If you're spending more time goofing off than you are studying, then it's best to part ways and plan to get together *after* the test.

Studying Alone

Even if you study with a group or a friend, it's important to spend time studying on your own, too. Here's why:

1. You can study at your own pace
2. You can study in your own way
3. You can spend extra time reviewing your special study areas
4. You have quiet and time to concentrate on the material

THE PLANETS IN THE SOLAR SYSTEM ARE...

SURVIVAL TIP:

Whether studying in a group, or alone, the key to learning the material is to review it, practice it, say it out loud, and quiz yourself!

CHEAT SHEET!

Sometimes it seems that no matter what you do, you just can't get stuff to sink in. Try these special tricks for remembering the tough stuff!

Technique	Example
Acronyms Use the first letter of each word you're trying to learn to make a sentence or a word that you can remember.	**HOMES** (The Great Lakes: **H**uron, **O**ntario, **M**ichigan, **E**rie, **S**uperior)
Picture This... Form a picture in your mind of what you're trying to learn. Make it HUGE: Visualize it larger than life Make it MOVE: Have action in your image Make it MANY: Don't just visualize one, visualize lots!	Giraffes are herbivores.
Association Link words you're trying to learn with something familiar.	**Rancid**—the smell of rotten milk
Rhyme Time Make up fun rhymes or simple songs.	"In 1492, Columbus sailed the ocean blue…"
Tell a Story Create a story where each word or idea you have to remember will cue the next idea you need to remember.	Christopher Columbus is a famous explorer. He is famous for his voyage in 1492. In 1492, he discovered America.

TEST DAY!

You've **studied hard**, had a **good night's sleep**, and eaten (a healthy) **breakfast**. You even had time to review your study sheet once more while waiting for the bus.

Six Simple Ways to Improve Your Grade

These six tips can help you do better—and they have nothing to do with how much you know!

1. Be Prepared

Arrive early so you have a few minutes to collect your thoughts and get focused on the test ahead. Arrange sharpened pencils, scratch paper, erasers, a calculator, or a ruler on your desk—or whatever tools you'll need.

2. Follow Directions

Listen to last-minute directions given by your teacher. They're likely to include important stuff you don't want to miss! When you get your test, **read** the directions *twice* and underline **key words** that explain what you should do. If you don't understand something, don't guess, **ask your teacher**.

3. Make a Plan

Take a moment to review the test to see how long it is and to plan how to best use your time. Don't waste time struggling with questions you don't know the answer to. Begin with the questions you *do* know. Save the questions you don't know until the end.

4. Brain Dump!
As soon as you get your test, jot down any stuff you're afraid of forgetting on the back, like important dates or tough equations.

5. Don't Act Too Fast
Read over *all* the answer choices before choosing. Even if you're sure you already spotted the right one, sometimes there's an *even better one* in the bunch!

6. Check Your Work
You've heard it a million times—review your work! Though you're sure you did it right the first time, you'll be amazed at what you may discover on a second read through. Use whatever time you have left at the end to check your test. After all, every point counts!

Panic Attack!

Everyone feels nervous before a test. A little bit of nerves can actually help motivate you. Too much can be a problem, especially if it interferes with your ability to perform well.

Try these tricks for handling test anxiety:

1. **Know your stuff!** Cramming for a test is a poor way to learn and can easily cause test anxiety. The more confident you are that you know the material, the less anxious you'll feel about doing well.

2. Remind yourself that a **test is only a test**! It isn't a measure of your self-worth, just a measure of what you've learned.

3. **Focus.** Concentrate on answering the question, not on the grade you'll get.

4. Take **deep breaths**. Not only will it help calm you, it also will send fresh oxygen to the brain to help it do its best!

Test Taking Tips

Use these strategies to help you with the toughest test questions!

TRUE OR FALSE?

1. Don't be fooled by a sentence that's only **partly true**. Carefully read each question and watch for anything that will make the statement false.

2. Be on the lookout for words like **"always"** or **"never."** Since few things in life are "always" or "never," they can be clues that the answer is false.

3. Watch out for words that tend to make a statement true, like **"usually"** or **"probably"** or **"some."**

Lucky Guess! What to do when you really don't know what to do...

If you really don't have a clue what the answer is, don't leave the question blank. Take a guess....Since the answer can only be true or false, you have a 50/50 chance of being right!

ESSAY QUESTION

1. Carefully read the question and look for key words that tell you what's wanted in your essay. Underline them.

2. Organize your thoughts before you write. Jot down a brief outline or notes on the back or side of the page to help guide you.

3. State your main points.

4. Provide examples in your essay to back up your main points.

5. End your essay with a **brief summary** that emphasizes your main points.

Lucky Guess! What to do when you really don't know what to do...

Do your best *not* to leave the question totally blank. Before you panic, take a moment to really think about the question. Is there any part of it you can answer? Any dates that relate? Places? People? Try to get something down that shows your teacher you have some understanding and knowledge of the info. Even a loosely constructed essay is better than no essay at all. Don't give up! Take a deep breath and do your best.

MULTIPLE CHOICE

1. **Before** looking at the choices, read the question and *answer* it in your head. Sometimes reading the choices first can cause you to jumble up the facts in your mind.

2. Read *all* your choices before answering. Even if you're sure the first answer is it, read on, there could be a *better* answer.

3. If you don't know the answer, use **process of elimination**. Narrow your choices down to two and make a guess.

4. When two very similar answers appear, there's a good chance that one of them is the correct choice. Teachers often disguise the right answer by giving another that is confusingly similar!

Lucky Guess! What to do when you really don't know what to do...

If you're down to a couple of choices, choose the answer that's longer and more descriptive. Teachers often give lots of description to help you identify the truth.

TICK-TOCK – TIME'S ALMOST UP!

You glance at the clock and realize you only have seven minutes left—what do you do when you have too much to do? Stop! Quickly scan your test and ask yourself these questions:

1. What sections are worth the most points?
2. What questions do I know the answers to?
3. How long will each section take me?

Do what you can to **earn the most points in the time you have left**. Answer the questions that you know the answers to and that won't take too long to complete. If you're struggling with an essay question that's worth 20 points, and the true/false section (which is easier for you) is worth the same, give up on the essay and switch to true/false.

Go for partial credit. Even if you don't have time to finish answering a question, teachers will often give some credit if you show that you know the stuff. Work out the first part of a math equation, or jot down any info that may relate to your essay topic.

WHEN YOU GET YOUR TEST BACK

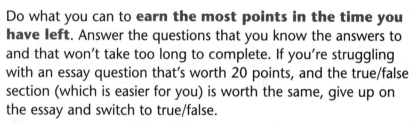

Don't just look at the grade and stuff your test in your knapsack. Go over what you got wrong so you can learn from your mistakes. When reviewing your test, ask yourself the following questions: Did I **follow the directions**? Is there a **pattern to my mistakes**?

Did I make **careless errors** that I could have caught if I had reread my work? Did I **run out of time**? Pay attention to the areas you need to brush up on and make sure you understand any questions you got wrong, so you can learn that material for next time. If necessary, **set up a meeting to go over your test** with your teacher.

Social Studies: Friends, Foes, and After-School Stuff

There's more to school than homework, classes, tests, and grades. School is also about **meeting people, making friends**, and **discovering things you like to do.** From sports teams to school plays, there are plenty of opportunities for getting involved—and meeting cool people along the way. But just like anything, even the fun, social side of school can have some bumps in its path. From **peer pressure** to **bullies**, this section is packed with tips to help you **survive** the social stuff!

GET INVOLVED

Getting involved in **school activities** is a great way to meet people with the same interests as you. It's also how you discover things that you like to do and are good at. From **after-school clubs** to **student government**, every school offers something. What do you like to do? Here are some ideas to get you thinking…

- if you're interested in **acting**, try out for the **school play**
- if you're interested in **singing**, think about joining the **chorus**

- if you love **sports**, try out for a **sports team**
- if you like to **write**, work on the **school newspaper**
- if you like to take **pictures**, join the **yearbook** staff
- if you're interested in **making a difference**, run for a **class office**

HELP! When you don't get chosen...

Whether it's for the play, the soccer team, or class president, the disappointment of not being picked can be huge. Remember these tips to help you survive:

1. Anytime you have to try out for something, **there's a chance you're not going to be selected**. There can be a lot of competition and more than one person can be right for the part or position. *Trying out or being elected is part of the process.*

2. Take a little time to be by yourself. Collect your thoughts and composure.

3. You certainly don't want to seem like a poor sport. **Congratulate** friends and classmates who *did* get selected.

4. Ask for suggestions on what you can do to improve your chances for when you try out next time.

5. Polish your skills. Do what you can to better your chances for getting a spot in the future.

The best way to make it is to **try again**!

Start Your Own Club!

Clubs are a great way to get together with old friends and make new ones. They're also a great way to spend time doing something you enjoy. Almost anything you like to do can make a great club. Follow these simple steps to start your own!

Step 1: Club Ideas

When choosing your club's theme, think about things you'd like to learn about or spend time doing. Write down a list of all your ideas and choose your favorite.

Step 2: Finding New Members

In addition to your buds, look for additional members outside your circle of friends. Make posters or fliers announcing your new club and the time, place, and date of the first meeting. Post them on bulletin boards at school and pass them out at lunch.

JOIN
The DOGWALKERS CLUB!
IF YOU LOVE DOGS AND WANT TO MAKE EXTRA $ COME TO OUR FIRST MEETING!
MONDAY DECEMBER 5 at 3:00 in the cafeteria
BRING FRIENDS!

Step 3: The First Meeting

If you plan on holding meetings at school, talk with your teacher about a good place to do so, and get permission. Other possible meeting places are someone's house or the public library. For most clubs, meeting once a week or every other week is enough. Sometimes, once a month will do.

Step 4: Club Notes and Other Important Info

Keep important stuff in a special club notebook. Make a list of things you want to talk about at each meeting. Use the notebook to take notes, record votes, and write down each member's name and phone number.

Step 5: A Job for All

Put everyone's talents to work. In your club notebook, write down a list of jobs, like president, vice president, secretary, or snack planner, and a list of their responsibilities. Have members volunteer, or hold an election and take a vote.

Step 6: Group Gripes

Let everyone have a say, and if the group can't agree, take a vote. You can raise your hands, or take a secret vote and write your decision on pieces of paper and have someone count them. If there's a tie, flip a coin and let that be the final decision.

SURVIVAL TIP:

Have fun! Make sure you have a plan for each meeting so people aren't bored. Keep your club busy with projects and activities.

Do It!

Here are some ideas to help you start your own club!

1. **Animal Lovers' Club:** Plan fun field trips to zoos, aquariums, and wildlife museums.
2. **Drama Club:** Write and put on your own plays.
3. **Camping Club:** Learn survival tricks, how to put up tents, and eat s'mores.
4. **Save the Environment Club:** Plant trees, pick up litter, and spread the word on recycling.
5. **Petsitters' Club:** Start a petsitting service and earn extra money.
6. **Charity Club:** Work together to raise money and donate it to a favorite charity—or charities.
7. **Bike Club:** Plan fun bike rides to take as a group.
8. **Sports Club:** Play your favorite sport and go to games.
9. **Book Club:** Read your favorite books and talk about them.
10. **Hobby Club:** Coin collecting, drawing, cooking—any hobby will make a great club.

CLIQUES AND PEER PRESSURE

There's nothing wrong with having a group of friends to hang out with. The important thing is not to let the group persuade you to lose sight of what's right. What would you do if caught in any of these situations?

"None of the popular kids at my school want to try out for the talent show. I want to, but I'm afraid if I do they'll think I'm a loser and I won't be popular anymore."

"My friends and I have a special table in the lunchroom that we eat at every day. When the new boy asked if he could sit with us, everyone said no, so he sat alone. I wanted to join him, but I knew my friends would make fun of me."

"There's a girl in my class who my friends tease. It makes me feel bad, but I go along with the group because I don't want them to pick on me instead."

"My friends think it's fun to steal candy from the store down the street. I don't like doing it, but they said if I didn't, I couldn't hang out with them anymore."

BE A LEADER, NOT A FOLLOWER!

the group is doing stuff that you know is **wrong** or **cruel**, hen it's time to **clique off!**

on't let the power of any "group" control you. If that little voice nside your head is saying that it's wrong, it probably is. The only erson responsible for your actions is you! So be true to yourself. **isten** to your head. **Follow** your heart. **Don't be afraid**

o tell others you on't agree with hem. If they get mad, ay you're sorry that our actions upset hem, but you don't ave to apologize or not joining in. our **real friends** ill respect you!

DEALING WITH BULLIES

ullies pick on others to make themselves feel powerful and mportant. Some are just looking for attention. Getting a eaction out of you can make bullies feel like they have the ower they want. Don't let ullies get the best of you! ere are some things to try if ou're being picked on.

. **Act brave and ignore the bully.** It's no fun to pick on someone if they don't react. Acting like you don't care may be enough to get the bully to back down. Eventually, the bully will get bored and move on.

2. Stand up for yourself. Simply say "please stop" and walk away.

3. Agree with the bully's insults. It's no fun to tease someone who isn't bothered by it.

4. Tell an adult. If the bullying is more than you can handle, or if the bully is physically hurting you, **talk to a teacher, principal, or parent immediately**. They can all help stop bullying.

Getting along with your classmates won't always be easy. Chances are you won't like everyone, and some kids won't like you, either. Being accepted by others is what most kids want. But understanding that others may not always like you is the first step to being happy and comfortable with yourself. Be true to yourself—and true friends will follow.

Help! "A girl in my class started a rumor about me. Now everyone laughs at me when I walk down the hall."

1. No matter what you say or do, **some people are going to believe the rumor**. Since you can't make *everyone* believe you, make it your goal to lessen the damage.

2. When you hear the rumor, don't freak, **play it cool**. If you over-react, people will think you actually *do* have something to hide. If you don't make a big deal out of it, others usually won't either.

3. **Laugh it off** and make a point of asking "Why would someone go to so much trouble to spread a lie?" This makes the person who started the rumor look like the foolish one!

4. Control the spread of the rumor **by spreading it yourself**. "Have you heard what's being said about me? What a joke!"

5. **Confront the person** who started the rumor. It's best to do this when you're calm and in private. Ask the person why she's spreading a lie about you and ask her to stop.

School's Out!

Or is it? Homework! There are **papers** to write, math **assignments** to finish, and **reading** to tackle. Check out these tips for helping you survive **homework**!

CHECK POINT

Before You Take Off At The End of the Day

Make sure you:

✔ check your assignment book so you know what you need to bring home

✔ pack up all of the books you'll need overnight

TOO MUCH TO DO? DON'T BITE OFF MORE THAN YOU CAN CHEW!

Do you have a problem **balancing** friends, homework, family, school, hobbies, sports, and all the *other* things that fill up the day? Lots of kids do because they **over-commit**. They fill up their schedule with too many after-school activities. The big question is how much can you *really* do and still get your homework done? **Planning** is the key to making a busy schedule work. To help you make the best use of your time, make an **after-school schedule** (see the next page). It will help you figure out what you have time for and what you don't!

Make an After-School Schedule

1. Start by filling in all the **things you *have* to do** like sports practice, music lessons, dinner, chores, and sleeping.

2. Now block out time for **homework**.

3. And finally—**free time!** This includes stuff like watching TV, reading just for fun, and hanging out with your family and friends.

Time	M	T	W	Th	F
3:00-4:00	Soccer Practice	Piano Practice	Soccer Practice	Student Council	Soccer Practice
4:00-5:00	Chores	FREE	Piano Practice	Piano Lesson	FREE
5:00-6:00	DINNER				
6:00-8:00	HOMEWORK				
8:00-9:00	FREE TIME!				
9:30	BEDTIME				

The Big Question...

Review your schedule and ask yourself: **Is my schedule balanced?**

Remember, you want to have a schedule that you can both **manage** and **enjoy**!

Along with all your activities, is there enough free time? What about family time? And of course, homework? If you feel worried that you've bitten off too much, **talk with your parent or teacher**. See if they can help you reorganize your schedule or help you figure out something to drop.

HOMEWORK!

Everybody who goes to school does **homework**. Teachers give homework not as torture (even though it might sometimes see like it!), but so you can **practice new skills** and **review others**. You can't escape it, hide from it, or pretend it doesn't exist. It'll follow you wherever you go. The only way to make homework disappear is to do it!

Smart Snacks

Before you sit down to study, energize your brain by eating a healthy snack. Skip the sugary stuff. It may give you a burst at first, but it will quickly make you tired or lose energy. Try these power boosts instead!

Dip It!

- Dip granola bars into yogurt. Set out a few different yogurt flavors to try.

- Dip apple slices into peanut (or cashew or almond) butter.

- Dip carrots and celery into your favorite salad dressing.

Tortilla Toppers

Spread the following combos on a tortilla, roll it up, and enjoy!

- Peanut butter and jelly topped with bananas

- Cream cheese topped with ham or turkey

- Spaghetti sauce topped with parmesan cheese

Frozen Fruits

- Insert a popsicle stick into a peeled banana. Put the banana on a plate and freeze it for at least one hour. For a tasty twist before you freeze the banana, drizzle it with honey and sprinkle it with shredded coconut, granola cereal, or chopped nuts.

- Put a bunch of frozen grapes in the freezer for at least one hour, then pop them in your mouth and enjoy.

HOMEWORK HELPERS

The only way to get your homework done is to do it! Try these tips to help you get the task done as painlessly as possible.

TIME CHECK

Check your **Personal Digital Assistant (PDA)** and the **after-school schedule** you made on page 61. Do your homework in the time slots you selected, and save the fun for when you're done.

DON'T DO HOMEWORK WHEN...

1. You're hungry

2. You're sleepy

3. You can't concentrate

Don't waste time wishing you were doing something else. Make sure you have a snack, take a quick nap if you need to, and grab short fifteen-minute breaks to help restore your concentration. Then get back to work!

PLACES, PLEASE

Try to have a **special place** where you do your homework every day. That way, when you sit down, your brain will automatically click into study mode. See page 10 for tips on creating a **study space** that works for you!

HARDEST FIRST

Tackle the **tough stuff first**, while your mind is still fresh. Save the easier assignments for later.

BREAK IT UP!

Take big assignments and **split** them into more **manageable chunks**. Look at your calendar and work back from the due date. Figure out how much you have to do each day to be finished by that date. Do it!

MINUTES MATTER

Do some homework while you're **riding on the bus, waiting to be picked up from play practice**, or in the **dentist's waiting room**. Lots of small chunks of time put together equal a big chunk of time! Make the most of it to get some homework done.

INTERMISSION

If you find yourself **spacing out** and **squirming** in your chair, **take a short break**. What's the point of sitting at your desk watching the time tick by and doing nothing? Set a break time, like **twenty minutes**. Then get up and stretch, walk the dog, or go for a bike ride. When you come back to your homework, your mind should be refreshed and ready to go.

REWARD YOURSELF!

Your homework is done and you deserve a reward! What fun things are you going to do when you finish your homework? Watch your favorite TV show? Go on a bike ride? Play with your new puppy? Call your best friend? With the work out of the way, your path is clear for play. Enjoy!

HOMEWORK HURDLES

The following problems are no excuse for not getting your homework done. Don't let them stop you!

Hurdle: I'm stuck!

Solution:
Don't give up! Check your **class notes** for clues, and review any readings that relate. If you're still stuck, **ask for help**. Perhaps a parent or sibling can guide you. If not, **call a classmate**—hopefully she can offer some assistance so you can get your work done. Or try a **homework helper website**, like:

Discoveryschool.com *(http://school.discovery.com/students)*
Ask Jeeves® Kids *(http://www.ajkids.com)*

Hurdle: I have too much homework!

Solution:
If you're having a problem finishing, take an honest look at your own homework habits. Are you **struggling with a certain subject** and it takes extra long to complete the work? Are you **distracted** by the TV in the background? Do you have too many after-school activities? Are you **putting off big assignments** until the last minute? The key to getting it done is to plan your time and use it wisely. Make and stick to your homework schedule (see page 61 to make one). Also try to set aside a certain amount of time to spend on each task, like 30 minutes. Then spend that time really focusing on the subject. Set the alarm on your **PDA** so you know when it's time to switch tasks. Use the PDA calendar to plan out long-term assignments so they don't creep up on you. If the work is really too hard, get **help from a parent or teacher**. Or ask for a tutor's help.

Hurdle: I left the book I need at school...

Solution:

If it's too late to go back to school, call a classmate and see if they can help you out. If he's finished with the book, maybe you can borrow it—if not for the evening, perhaps long enough to get the info you need copied on a copy machine. But the best solution is prevention! Don't rely on your memory when packing up to go home. Take the time to check your assignment book or **PDA** before you leave school. Check each item off as you put it in your bag to take home.

Hurdle: I didn't get the assignment because I was out sick...

Solution:

Being sick isn't going to get you out of homework! Most teachers consider it your responsibility to find out what you missed and make up the work once you're well. Call a classmate to find out what you missed. Have a sibling or friend bring home any books or handouts you may need.

 **Help! "The dog ate my homework…"**

1. Dogs don't eat homework and teachers know it! Whether you have a good reason for not doing your homework, like you were sick, or you have no reason at all, like you just wanted to watch TV, your best bet is to tell your teacher the **truth**. Telling the truth doesn't get you off—it just helps you save face! If there's a good reason why you didn't do it, **have a parent write a note** explaining the situation.

2. If you don't have a good reason for not getting it done, **take a look at your attitude**. It's almost impossible to be successful at school if you don't do your homework. Everyone gets behind sometimes, but the key is to get yourself out of the hole *before* you're in too deep!

I'M SORRY I DIDN'T DO MY HOMEWORK, BUT I WASN'T FEELING GOOD. AFTER DINNER. HERE'S A NOTE FROM MY MOM

READING

Many students open their books, read until they finish, and consider the assignment done. But just because your eyes soaked up the words doesn't mean your brain did! Did you

understand what you read? Do you remember it? Being a **good reader** takes **concentration**. Read on for tips to help you get the reading to sink in and stick.

1. Preview

Take a moment to scan the material before you start reading. How long is it? What's it about? Read the headings. Knowing what the reading is going to be about *before* you start will help prepare you for what you're about to learn.

2. Get a Clue

Textbooks often have questions at the end of each chapter. Reviewing them *before* you start reading will alert you to the important stuff you should be on the lookout for.

3. Baby Bites

How long can you read and truly concentrate? If you have a long reading assignment, break it into pieces and read just a bit at a time. Then take a break and do something else. Come back to it when your mind is revived.

4. Be Active!

Taking part in your reading will help you concentrate. Use a highlighter to underline important stuff. Put a star by anything super important you want to make sure to remember, and a question mark by anything you don't understand. If the book isn't yours, take notes on a piece of paper. Write down important stuff and any questions you may have. Or mark important pages with sticky notes that you can remove when it's time to return the book. Make brief notes on the stickies to remind yourself why you marked the page.

5. The End

You've finished the reading, but did it sink in? Test yourself by using your own words to summarize what the reading was about. If you can't, you better read it again!

WRITING

Book reports, research papers, essays—writing assignments can have many purposes, but the basic structure is the same. Don't let the thought of putting pen to paper intimidate you—if you follow a few simple steps, you'll find that your paper will almost write itself! Well, maybe not quite!

This next section is full of tips to help you turn your ideas into sentences, and your sentences into great papers!

Don't Procrastinate!

It's very easy to put off long papers until right before they're due. Don't let time creep up on you! Not only will the quality of your paper suffer, but having to pack lots of work into a short period of time is guaranteed to make the experience miserable. Try to start the day your teacher gives the assignment. Use the calendar on your **PDA** to help you organize

your time. Work back from the due date and figure out how long it will take you to complete each of the following six steps. Stick to your timeline!

SIX STEPS TO A GREAT PAPER

To help you organize your time, and make the job more manageable, break the project into pieces. Then focus on accomplishing one step at a time.

STEP 1: SELECT A TOPIC

What are you going to write about? In some cases, your teacher will have assigned a specific topic. Other times you'll be free to choose. Having to choose your own topic can make the task of getting started seem even harder. Here's the good news—you can write about something that's interesting to you! To help you come up with a list of ideas, **brainstorm**.

Places I'd Like to See
- Dodger Stadium
- Grand Canyon
- O'Hare Airport
- Hawaiian Volcano
- Cookie Factory

To get started, jot down:

    1. Your favorite things to do

    2. Things you'd like to learn about

    3. Places you'd like to see

    4. Famous people you'd like to meet

    5. A moment in history you'd like to experience

Review your list for a topic that fits the requirements. It may not be obvious at first, but one of your ideas can probably be molded to fit the assignment.

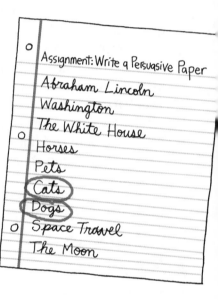

Assignment: Write a Persuasive Paper
Abraham Lincoln
Washington
The White House
Horses
Pets
Cats
Dogs
Space Travel
The Moon

STEP 2: RESEARCH

Now that you have your topic, it's time to start gathering the facts. Don't just rely on one source for all your info—try to use a variety of sources. Here are some good places to look:

INFORMATION

✔ **Library:** Ask a librarian to help you get started in your search. From finding newspaper archives to book titles, the librarian can give you lots of good tips!

✔ **Books:** Always a good reliable source of info.

A-F G-M N-T U-Z

✔ **Encyclopedias:** Great for finding general stuff and getting an overview of your subject.

✔ **Magazines & Newspaper Archives:** Offer specific stories and true events.

✔ **Videos and DVDs:** Packed with info and fun to watch. Make sure to take good notes!

✔ **Museums:** If there's one in your area, check to see if there are any specific exhibits that relate to your topic.

✔ **Interviews:** Put a list of questions together and talk to a pro.

✔ **Internet:** Type your subject into a search engine and see what pops up. Online encyclopedias are also a good and reliable source of info. Print out any helpful stuff you may want to use. Make sure your Internet source is a reliable one—use stuff offered by established organizations instead of unknown individuals.

SURVIVAL TIP:

Keep a list of all the sources you use. Write down the title, author, and publisher. That way if anyone asks where you got something from, or if you have to go back to the source, you'll have it.

STEP 3: ORGANIZE YOUR IDEAS

Now that you've gathered your facts, create a simple outline of your paper. It will make the writing process much easier if you've organized your ideas before you start! Here's what you do:

1. Write your topic at the top of the page.

2. Each paragraph in your paper gets a Roman numeral. Next to each Roman numeral, write the main point of the paragraph.

3. Under each paragraph, list the facts that support the main idea. Label these with letters.

4. Give examples to support each fact. Label these with regular numbers.

Why Cats Make Great Pets

I. Dogs are not the only pets people enjoy

   A. For many people, a cat is their best friend

   B. Despite what dog lovers believe, cats make great house pets

II. People enjoy the companionship of cats

   A. Cats are affectionate and playful

     1. like to snuggle

     2. like to chase balls

   B. Cats are civilized and can be trained

STEP 4: WRITE YOUR INTRODUCTORY PARAGRAPH

The intro paragraph is the first one of your paper. It introduces the main idea of your essay and should capture the reader's interest. The main idea of the paper is stated in a single sentence. All the info you present in your paper will back up and support this one idea. Look at your outline and decide what the main point you will be making is. Your main idea should be the last sentence of the intro paragraph.

There is an old saying that "dogs are a man's best friend." Dogs are not the only animal whose companionship people enjoy. For many, a cat is their best friend. Despite what some dog lovers believe, cats make great house pets.

Main Idea

STEP 5: SUPPORTING PARAGRAPHS

Supporting paragraphs make up the main body of your essay. Each supporting paragraph should help you prove the point you're making. Like all good paragraphs, supporting paragraphs should have sentences that give facts, details and examples backing up the main sentence.

Cats are affectionate. They like to snuggle and be scratched behind the ears. They will curl up in your lap and take a nap. They also purr when you pet them. Who can resist a purring cat?

Cats are also playful. They like to chase balls, bells, and hit at anything dangling on a string. They really like playing with their owners.

STEP 6: THE CONCLUSION

The conclusion is the last paragraph of your essay. It should summarize or restate the main points, or briefly describe your feelings about the topic.

Cats are low maintenance, civilized companions. They are affectionate, playful, and clean. They also make very little noise and don't bark. In many ways, cats are ideal house pets.

REREADING AND REVISING

One of the most important things you can do to improve your grade is to take the time to carefully read your paper before you turn it in. Look at your paragraphs and ask yourself the following questions:

1. Do I have a main idea?

2. Does my paper support my main idea?

3. Are my sentences clearly written? Do they flow smoothly?

Keep your eyes open for ways to improve your paper. The first draft is rarely good enough to turn in for a grade. Once you get the words down, you're likely to find a bunch of ways to make your paper even better. It's called *revising*, and it's an important part of the writing process. It's what turns a good paper into a great paper!

PRESENTATION

Even papers make a first impression! Make sure yours is a good one by using the following checklist.

☐ Have you created a title page with your name, date, class, and paper title?

☐ Have you spell-checked and grammar-checked? (They won't catch every error, but they might catch errors you've missed.)

☐ Have you numbered the pages?

☐ Did you double space your lines?

☐ Is your work printed on clean, white paper?

☐ Is your paper in a report cover or stapled together?

When typing your paper on a computer, remember to

1. Save your work often so it doesn't get lost!

2. Back up your work! Print out drafts as you go along and save your info on a disk.

Why Cats Make Great Pets
Amanda Zimmer
English   December 1

QUICK TIP GRAMMAR GUIDE

Stumped? Use this basic guide to help solve your punctuation problems!

Punctuation Mark	Use	Example
?	Use a question mark at the end of a sentence to show a direct question.	What is your favorite food?
!	Use an exclamation point to show excitement or surprise.	I love hot dogs!
.	Use a period to show the end of a sentence.	Hot dogs are my favorite food.
,	Use a comma to show a pause in a sentence.	Since Sammy loves hot dogs, his mom is planning to serve them at the party.
	Use a comma for listing three or more different things.	Sammy's mom served hot dogs, potato chips, and cake.
	Use commas around clauses that add extra information to a sentence.	Sammy's mom, who hosted the party, makes great hot dogs.
" "	Use quotation marks when using somebody else's words.	When I asked Sammy what his favorite food is, he answered, "I love hot dogs!"
	Use quotation marks to show that someone is speaking.	"I love hot dogs," said Sammy.

WORDS TO WATCH OUT FOR!

These commonly confused words are the kind of mistakes spell check can't detect! Can you?

When to use...	Definition	Example
it's, its	*It's* is the short form of "it is". *Its* is a pronoun that shows ownership or possession of.	**It's** in the car. That car has a mind of **its** own.
than, then	*Than* means in "comparison with". *Then* means "next".	He is stronger **than** me. First I went to the candy store, and **then** I went to the library.
their, there, they're	*Their* is a form of "they" that shows ownership. *There* describes where something is. *They're* is the short form of "they are".	**Their** tree house is so cool. The car keys are over **there**. **They're** going to let me go home early.
to, too	*To* means "in the direction of". *Too* means "also or besides". *Too* can also mean excess.	My family went **to** the airport. My friend came along to the airport, **too**. He ate **too** much candy during the movie.
your, you're	*Your* is a form of "you" that shows ownership. *You're* is the short form of "you are".	**Your** dog is cute. **You're** so lucky to have such a cute dog.

POP QUIZ — SPELLING BEE CHALLENGE

Can you correctly spell these frequently misspelled words? They are all misspelled here. Buzz on over to the answer key on the next page to see how you did!

1. **welcom**

2. **bigest**

3. **acomplish**

4. **beleve**

5. **desert** *(like ice cream)*

6. **truely**

7. **embaras**

8. **goverment**

9. **grammer**

10. **exsided**

11. **geting**

12. **begining**

13. **particuler**

14. **tomatos**

15. **potatos**

16. **solveing**

17. **recomend**

18. **scarey**

19. **succes**

20. **spagetti**

AND FINALLY...

CHECK POINT

Before Going to Bed

Pack up everything you need for school the next day, like:

✔ finished homework

✔ books

✔ plenty of paper and sharpened pencils or pens

✔ lunch or lunch money

✔ signed permission slip, if you have one

✔ sneakers or gym clothes

Answer Key

1. **welcome**	11. **getting**
2. **biggest**	12. **beginning**
3. **accomplish**	13. **particular**
4. **believe**	14. **tomatoes**
5. **dessert**	15. **potatoes**
6. **truly**	16. **solving**
7. **embarrass**	17. **recommend**
8. **government**	18. **scary**
9. **grammar**	19. **success**
10. **excited**	20. **spaghetti**

Survival Secrets of Successful Students...

Anyone can be successful at school and have fun doing it! As you learned by reading this book, you don't have to be a genius, but you *do* have to be dedicated— you have to try! To sum it all up:

- **Have a winning attitude** and plan to succeed!
- **Have a plan** and work to achieve it.
- **Don't bite off more than you can chew.** Make sure you have a balanced schedule that you can manage and enjoy.
- **Don't procrastinate.** Just do it!
- **Take care of yourself.** Get a good night's sleep so you can be sharp. Fuel your body and brain with healthy foods.
- **Participate.** From class discussions to group projects, being involved helps you learn.
- **Take part in extracurricular activities.** School isn't just about classes and grades. It's also about trying new things, discovering what you're good at, and having fun!
- **Have school spirit!** Give it your all!

And by coming to the end of this book, you now know how to **master the school universe**! The rest is up to you. Armed with this book, the techniques you learned by reading it, and your go-get-'em-attitude, you should now feel confident that you can **survive**, succeed in, and enjoy **school**!